A LAP OF HONOUR

HUGH MacDIARMID

A Lap of Honour

MACGIBBON & KEE

FIRST PUBLISHED 1967 BY MACGIBBON AND KEE LTD
1–3 UPPER JAMES STREET LONDON WI
COPYRIGHT © CHRISTOPHER MURRAY GRIEVE 1967
PRINTED IN GREAT BRITAIN BY
EBENEZER BAYLIS AND SON LTD
THE TRINITY PRESS
WORCESTER AND LONDON

ACKNOWLEDGEMENTS

THE POEMS in this collection appeared in the following magazines and volumes: 'By Wauchopeside' (*The Modern Scot*); 'Diamond Body' (*The Welsh Review*); 'Prayer for a Second Flood' (*First Hymn to Lenin and other poems*, Unicorn Press); 'Whuchulls' (*The Modern Scot*); 'The Burning Passion' (*First Hymn to Lenin and other poems*, Unicorn Press); 'The Terrible Crystal' (*The Poetry Review*); 'A Vision of Scotland' (*The Poetry Review*); 'Larking Dallier' (*The London Mercury*); 'Esplumeoir' (*Honour'd Shade. An Anthology*, Chambers); 'On a Raised Beach' (*Stony Limits and other poems*, Gollancz); 'In Talk with Donnchadh Bàn Mac an T'Saoir' (*New Poems 1953. A P.E.N. Anthology*, Joseph); 'Once in a Cornish Garden' (*Botteghe Oscure*); 'Depth and the Chthonian Image' (*Scots Unbound and other poems*, Eneas Mackay); 'The Royal Stag' (*Scottish Eccentrics*, Routledge, 1936).

CONTENTS

PREFATORY NOTE

THE TITLE I have chosen for this collection of my poems seems appropriate. My *Collected Poems* was published in 1962: but the title was a misnomer. The MSS I sent in to the publishers of that book was much too large for their purpose and only a portion of it was used. The poems in this volume, however, did not, (save for a short out-of-context extract, from 'On a Raised Beach') appear in that collection, nor even in the discarded large part of the original MSS sent in. The fact is that I had quite forgotten having written many of these poems, and owe their recovery now to my friend Mr Duncan Glen, whose book on my work, *Hugh MacDiarmid and the Scottish Renaissance* (Chambers, Edinburgh) was published in 1964.

In the introduction to my *Collected Poems* it is stated that it contains all the poems I still approved. That introduction was, however, written for the larger collection and unfortunately was not altered when only a part of that was published. So it is not the case that I ever considered the poems here unworthy of republication.

On the contrary. The present book contains some of my best poems both in English and in Scots. With regard to the latter in particular, it is believed in some quarters that in recent years I have ceased to write in the aggrandised Scots in which I wrote my early lyrics in the 'Twenties. The fact is that after the success of these I, like Heine after the success of his lyrics, found (as the late Professor Laura Hofrichter brings out so convincingly in her book on the subject) I could no longer go on with that sort of thing but required to break up the unity of the lyric and introduce new material of various kinds on different levels of significance. It took Heine years of agonised effort to find the new form he needed, and his later work, in which he did find it, never won a measure of esteem like that secured by his early work. So it is in my case. But poems like 'Wauchopeside' and 'Whuchulls' succeed, I believe, in realising the sort of poem in Scots I wanted when I ceased to write the kind of short lyric on which my reputation was at first based.

I am now seventy-five, and cannot therefore promise that there will be any substantial further addition to the corpus of my poetry, except for my very long, unpublished, and still uncompleted 'Impavidi Progrediamur', to which, however, I will, instead of that Latin title, give the Scots one of 'Haud Forrit'.

Biggar, 1967   HUGH MACDIARMID

A LAP OF HONOUR

BY WAUCHOPESIDE

THRAWN water? Aye, owre thrawn to be aye thrawn!
I ha'e my wagtails like the Wauchope tae,
Birds fu' o' fechtin' spirit, and o' fun,
That whiles jig in the air in lichtsome play
Like glass-ba's on a fountain, syne stand still
Save for a quiver, shoot up an inch or twa, fa' back
Like a swarm o' winter-gnats, or are tost aside,
        By their inclination's kittle loup,
        To balance efter hauf a coup.

There's mair in birds than men ha'e faddomed yet.
Tho' maist churn oot the stock sangs o' their kind
There's aiblins genius here and there; and aince
'Mang whitebeams, hollies, siller birks—
        The tree o' licht—
            I mind
I used to hear a blackie mony a nicht
Singin' awa' t'an unconscionable 'oor
Wi' nocht but the water keepin't company
(Or nocht that ony human ear could hear)
—And wondered if the blackie heard it either
Or cared whether it was singin' tae or no'!
O there's nae sayin' what my verses awn
To memories like these. Ha'e I come back
To find oot? Or to borrow mair? Or see
Their helpless puirness to what gar'd them be?
        Late sang the blackie but it stopt at last.
        The river still ga'ed singin' past.

O there's nae sayin' what my verses awn
To memories, or my memories to me.
But a'e thing's certain; ev'n as things stand
I could vary them in coontless ways and gi'e
Wauchope a new course in the minds o' men,
The blackie gowden feathers, and the like,
An yet no' cease to be dependent on

15

The things o' Nature, and create insteid
Oot o' my ain heid
Or get ootside the range
O' trivial change
Into that cataclysmic country which
Natheless a' men inhabit—and enrich.

For civilization in its struggle up
Has mair than seasonal changes o' ideas,
Glidin' through periods o' flooers and fruit,
Winter and Spring again; to cope wi' these
Is difficult eneuch to tax the patience
O' Methuselah himsel'—but transformations,
Yont physical and mental habits, symbols, rites,
That mak' sic changes nane, are aye gaen on,
Revolutions in the dynasty o' live ideals
—The stuff wi' which alane true poetry deals.
Wagtail or water winna help me here,
(That's clearer than Wauchope at its clearest's clear!)
Where the life o' a million years is seen
Like a louch look in a lass's een.

NOTE: Wauchope is one of the tributaries of the River Esk, which it joins at
the little Dumfriesshire town of Langholm, the author's birthplace.

DIAMOND BODY

IN A CAVE OF THE SEA

WHAT after all do we know of this terrible 'matter'
Save as a name for the unknown and hypothetical cause
Of states of our own consciousness? There are not two worlds,
A world of nature, and a world of human consciousness,
Standing over against one another, but one world of nature
Whereof human consciousness is an evolution,
I reminded myself again as I caught that sudden breathless glimpse,
Under my microscope, of unexpected beauty and dynamic living
In the world of life on a sliver of kelp
Quite as much as the harpooning of a forty-two foot whale shark.

Because, I reminded myself, any assemblage of things
Is for the sake of another, and because of
The existence of active exertion
For the sake of abstraction,
In like manner, as Gaudapada says,
As a bed, which is an assemblage
Of bedding, props, cotton, coverlet, and pillows
Is for another's use, not for its own
And its several component parts
Render no mutual service,
Thence it is concluded that there is a man
Who sleeps upon the bed
And for whose sake it was made
So this world, which is an assemblage
Of the five elements is for another's use,
And there is another for whose enjoyment
This enjoyable body of mine,
Consisting of intellect and all the rest,
Has been produced.

And all I see and delight in now
Has been produced for him—
The sand-burrowing sea urchins with shells

2

Delicate as those of hen's eggs,
Burrowing by movements of long backwardly-directed spines;
And the burrowing star-fish which settle into the sand
By rows of pointed 'tube feet',
Operated by hydraulic pressure,
On the under-side of each of the five arms;
And the smooth-bodied sand eels and the shrimps
And sea-weeds attached by broad hold-fasts
—Not roots!—to the rocks or boulders,
Brown masses a host of small animals
Grow on or shelter amongst, protected here
From the buffeting of the sea when the tide is in
Or kept moist under the damp weight of weed
When the tide is out. And high up the shore
The limpets wandering about
Grazing on fine encrusting weeds,
And the acorn barnacles, the dog-whelks
Grey-shelled unless they have mussels to feed on
When the change of diet puts brown bands on the shells;
And, in a rock pool, 'crumb of bread' sponge,
Hydroids red, green, purple, or richly patterned
Like the dahlia anemone, yellow sea-lemon, and now and again
A rapidly moving snail shell which shows me
It is inhabited by a hermit crab
Much more active than its original occupant.
Countless millions of creatures each essential
To that other, and precisely fashioned
In every detail to meet his requirements.
Millions upon millions of them
Hardly discernible here
In the brilliant light in which sea and sky
Can hardly be distinguished from each other
—And I know there are billions more
Too small for a man to see
Even though human life were long enough
To see them all, a process that can hardly
Be even begun.
Our minds already sense that the fabric of nature's laws
Conceals something that lies behind it,

A greater-unity.—We are beginning more and more
To see behind them something they conceal
For the most part cunningly
With their outward appearances,
By hoodwinking man with a façade
Quite different from what it actually covers.
I am convinced that behind this too
There is another and many more.
Today we are breaking up the chaste
Ever-deceptive phenomena of Nature
And reassembling them according to our will.
We look through matter, and the day is not far distant
When we shall be able to cleave
Through her oscillating mass as if it were air.[1]
Matter is something which man still
At most tolerates, but does not recognise.
Here in the brilliant light, where the mandala[2] is almost complete,
The circumference of a blinding diamond broken
Only by a few points and dashes of darkness yet,
The shapes and figures created by the fire of the spirit
Are only empty forms and colours. It is not necessary to confuse
The dull glow of such figures with the pure white light
Of the divine body of truth, nor to project
The light of the highest consciousness into concretized figures,
But to have the consciousness withdrawn, as if
To some sphere beyond the world where it is

[1] *Vide* the Aphorisms of Franz Marc.

[2] In 'The Secret of the Golden Flower', symbols having the form of mandalas are reproduced. Mandala means circle, specifically 'magic circle': (Jung has published the mandalas of a somnambulist in his *Collecting Papers on Analytical Psychology*). Magic, because the protecting figure of the enclosing circle is supposed to prevent any 'out-pouring', that, is, to prevent consciousness being burst asunder by the unconscious, or by partial psychical systems—complexes split off from the whole. At the same time, the mandala gives form to the transformation of inward feeling, such as Paul, for instance, has in mind when he recognizes that 'it is not I who live, but Christ who lives in me'—Christ being here the symbol of the mystical fact of transformation. The inner conversion, the assumption of a unique individuality, is described by the Chinese as the production of the 'diamond body' or the 'sacred fruit'.

At once empty and not empty,
The centre of gravity of the whole personality
Transferred from the conscious centre of the ego
To a sort of hypothetical point
Between the conscious and the unconscious,
The complete abolition of the original
Undifferentiated state of subject and object;
Thus through the certainty that *something lives through me*
Rather than I myself live[3]
A man bridges the gap between instinct and spirit,
And takes hold upon life, attacks life,
In a more profound sense than before.
In the reconciliation of the differentiated
And the inferior function, the 'great Tao
—The meaning of the world' is discovered.

Crossing the island I see the tail of my coat
Wave back and forth and know
It is the waves of the sea on my beach.
And now I am in the cave. A moment ago
I saw the broad leather-brown belts of the tangleweed,
And the minute forms that fix themselves
In soft carmine lace-stencils upon the shingle,
The notched wrack gemmed with lime-white bead-shells
Showing like pearls on a dark braid,
And minute life in a million forms.
And I saw the tide come crawling
Through the rocky labyrinths of approach
With flux and reflux—making inch upon inch
In an almost imperceptible progress.
But now I know it is the earth
And not the water that is unstable,
For at every rise and fall of the pellucid tide
It seems as though it were the shingle
And the waving forest of sea-growth
That moves—and not the water!

[3] See 'The Secret of the Golden Flower', a Chinese *Book of Life*, translated into German and annotated by Richard Wilhelm with a European commentary by C. G. Jung.

And, after all, there is no illusion,
But seeming deception prefigures truth,
For it is a matter of physiographical knowledge
That in the long passages of time
The water remains—and the land ebbs and flows.

I have achieved the diamond body.

PRAYER FOR A SECOND FLOOD

THERE'D ha'e to be nae warnin'. Times ha'e changed
And Noahs are owre numerous nooadays,
(And them the vera folk to benefit maist!)
Knock the feet frae under them, O Lord, wha praise
Your unsearchable ways sae muckle and yet hope
        To keep within knowledgeable scope!

Ding a' their trumpery show to blauds again.
Their measure is the thimblefu' o' Esk in spate.
Like whisky the tittlin' craturs mete oot your poo'ers
Aince a week for bawbees in the kirk-door plate,
—And pit their umbrellas up when they come oot
        If mair than a pulpitfu' o' You's aboot!

O arselins wi' them! Whummle them again!
Coup them heels-owre-gowdy in a storm sae gundy
That mony a lang fog-theekit face I ken
'll be sooked richt doon under through a cundy
In the High Street, afore you get weel-sterted
        And are still hauf-herted!

Then flush the world in earnest. Let yoursel' gang,
Scour't to the bones, and mak' its marrow holes
Toom as a whistle as they used to be
In days I mind ere men fidged wi' souls,
But naething had forgotten you as yet,
        Nor you forgotten it.

Up then and at them, ye Gairds o' Heaven.
The Divine Retreat is owre. Like a tidal bore
Boil in among them; let the lang lugs nourished
On the milk o' the word at last hear the roar
O' human shingle; and replenish the salt o' the earth
        In the place o' their birth.

WHUCHULLS[1]

'Il ne peut y avoir du progrès (vrai, c'est-à dire moral), que dans l'individu et par l'individu lui-même.'—Charles Baudelaire

Gie owre your coontin, for nae man can tell
The population o' a wud like this
In plants and beasts, and needna pride himsel'
On ocht he marks by a' he's boond to miss.
What is oor life that we should prize't abune
Lichen's or slug's o' which we ken scarce mair
Than they o' oors when a' thing's said and dune,
Or fancy it ser's 'heicher purposes'?
The wice man kens that a fool's brain and his
Differ at maist as little 'gainst a' that is
As different continents and centuries,
Time, station, caste, culture, or character—
Triflin' distinctions that dinna cairry faur—
And if at ony point he stops and says:
'My lot has fa'n in mair enlightened days,
I'm glad to be a European, no' a black
—Human, no' hotchin' glaur ahint his back
Let him forehear as foolish a future set
Him in a class as seemin' laicher yet,
Or ten pasts damn him for a graceless get.
Original forest, Whuchulls, public park,
Mysel', or ony man, beast, mineral, weed,
I clearly see are a' aside the mark.
The poet hauds nae brief for ony kind,
Age, place, or range o' sense, and no' confined
To ony nature can share Creation's insteed.
First speir this bowzie bourach if 't prefers
The simmer or the winter, day or night,
New or forhooied nests, rain's pelts or smirrs,
Bare sticks or gorded fullyery; and syne invite
My choice twixt good and evil, life and death.

[1] Local pronunciation of Whitshiels, a wood near Langholm.

What hoar trunk girds at ivy or at fug
Or what sleek bole complains it lacks them baith?
Nae foliage hustle-farrant in windy light
Is to the Muse a mair inspirin' sight
Than fungus poxy as the mune; nae blight
A meaner state than flourish at its height.
Leafs' music weel accords wi' gloghole's glug.
Then cite nae mair this, that, or onything.
To nae belief or preference I cling,
Earth—let alane the mucklest mountain in't—
Is faur owre kittle a thing to scho ahint.
I'll no' toy wi' the fragments o't I ken
—Nor seek to beshield *it*, least o' a' men!...
Yet here's a poem takin' shape again,
Inevitable shape, faur mair inevitable
Than birks and no' bamboos or banyans here,
Impredictable, relentless, thriddin' the rabble
O' themes and aspects in this thrawart scene.
O freedom constrainin' me as nae man's been
Mair constrained wha wasna, as I'll yet be, freer!...

Clearlier it comes. I winna ha'e it. Quick
And gi'e me tutors in arboriculture then.
Let me plunge where the undergrowth's mair thick.
Experts in forestry, botany—a' that ken
Mair than I dae o' onything that's here.
I ken sae little it easily works its will.
Fence me frae its design wi' endless lear.
Pile up the facts and let me faurer ben.
Multiply my vocabulary ten times ten.
Let me range owre a' prosody again.
Mak' yon a lammergeir, no' juist a wren.
Is that owre muckle for a Scotsman yet,
Needin' a soupler leid, great skills, he lacks?
Is he in silence safer frae attacks?
Yet wha can thole to see it cavalierly choose
In God's green wud—tak' this and that refuse?
Yon knoul-taed trees, this knurl, at least 't'll use!
Gar memory gie the place fower seasons at aince.'

The world's no' mine. I'll tak' nae hen's care o't.
'*Is that Creation's nature you evince,*
Sma-bookin' Whuchulls to a rice or twa
Sae arbirtrarily picked, and voidin' a'
The lave as gin it wasna worth a jot?'

There is nae reason but on unreason's based
And needs to mind that often to hain its sense,
Dodo and Mammoth had the same misplaced
Trust in their *données*—and hae lang gane hence.
Why fash sae muckle owre Nature's present stock
In view o' a' past changes and to come?
It's wipin' oot 'ud be nae greater shock
Than mony afore; and Poetry isna some
Society for Preservin' Threatened Types,
But strokes a cat or fiddles on its tripes,
And for inclusions or exclusions, fegs,
Needna apologize while a'e bird's eggs
Are plain, anither's speckled, beasts ha'e legs,
Birds wings, Earth here brairds trees, here nocht but seggs.
'Troth it's an insult for a man to seek
A'e woman owre anither. A' women hae
Their differences and resemblances, but whatna freak
Thinks, frae the latter, ony ane'll dae
Or, frae the former, fain 'ud sair them a'?

The world o' a' the senses is the same.
Creation disna live frae hand to mooth
Juist improvisin' as it gangs, forsooth,
And there's nae meanin' in life that bode to da'
Until we came—or bides a wicer day—
'Yont brute creation, fools, bairns, unborn, deid.
I'd sing bird-mooth'd wi' ony ither creed,
No' wi' Creation's nature and its aim;
Or sing like Miffy—wheesht, world, while he speaks.
In English—hence, the Universal Speech.
He has nae wings; let birds pit on the breeks.
Nae fins. Fish, copy him! And sae let each
O' Nature's sorts be modelled upon him

Frae animalculae to Seraphim.
He is nae poet, but likes the Laureate best.
What, write like that?—Ah! here's the crucial test!
I ha'e the courage to be a Scotsman then
(Nae Scot 'll e'er be Laureate we ken!)[1]
Divided frae ither folk to Eternity's en',
And, if I hadna, ken it wadna maitter.
I'd be it still. Exclusive forms are nature.
It means to be and comes in Nature's way.
—*In its ain nature's, as a' in Nature does.*
Supersessions, innovations, variations, display
Nature, no' hide; and Scotland, Whuchulls, us
Interest me less for what they are than as
Facts o' the creative poo'er that, tho' they pass,
'll aye be qualified by their ha'en been.
It is nae treason then to stell my een
No' on their fleetin' shapes but on their deep
Constituent principles destined to keep
A mystery greater than the sight o' eels
Kelterin' through a' the seven seas reveals.
These to a'e spot converge, but we gang oot
Aye faurer frae oor source—ne'er back, I doot.
'*I like to see the ramel gowd-bestreik,*
And sclaffer cuit-deep through the birsled leafs.
Here I dung doon the squirrels wi' my sling
And made the lassies brooches o' their paws,
Set girns for rabbits and for arnuts socht,
Herried my nests and blew the eggs, and lit
Fires o' fir-burrs and hag in tinker style.
Hoo faur the interests a' progress warrant
Meddlin' wi' Whuchulls' auld amenities,
And their dependent livelihoods and ploys,
I'm no' to say; I'm glad to see it still
Temporarily triumphant against control.
It's pleasant nae doot for a woman to dream
O' yieldin' hersel' to some buirdly man
Wha kens what he wants and willy-nilly'll ha'e't
But when the time comes she'll aye find, I think,

[1] 'There are poets little enough to envy even a poet-laureate.'—*Gray.*

Guid reasons for no' yieldin'—bless her hert!
Sae wi' the Whuchulls. May the Lord be praised.'
Nae doot primeval beasts felt juist the same
Aboot the place—tho' different frae this
As ony change that's still in store for it.
Hauf saurian-emeritus, hauf prentice spook,
You'll never see the plantin' for the trees,
This Eden where Adam comes fu' circle yet.

There is nae ither way. For weel or woe
It is attained. Tho' idle side-winds blow
In on me still and inferior questions thraw
Their crockets up, a' doots and torments cease.
The road is clear. I gang in perfect peace,
And my idea spreids and shines and lures me on,
O lyric licht auld chaos canna dam!
Celestial, soothin', sanctifyin' course, wi' a'
The high sane forces o' the sacred time
Fechtin' on my side through it till I con
This blainy blanderin' and ken that I'm
Delivered frae the need o' trauchlin' wi't,
Accommodated to't, but in my benmaist hert
Acknowledgmentless, free, condition or reform,
Or sunny lown or devastatin' storm,
Indifferent to me; where the Arts stert
Wi' a' else *corpore vili*—'*God's mercy-seat!*'

THE BURNING PASSION

(For Carmel Haden Guest)

'From Homer and Polygnotus I every day learn more clearly that in our life here above ground we have, properly speaking, to enact Hell.' (*Briefwechsel zwischen Schiller und Goethe* VI 230).

WAD that the burnin' passion aince attained
Whether by lichtnin' flash or creepin' dawn
Nae langer came and gaed but held for aye,
Wi'ts growth, gin Change is needfu' still to Man,
Ha'sein' us in, no' o', perfection
  Its haill direction.

But oh! The apathy that fixes on
Men wha accordin' to the spirit live
—The constant problem o' recapturin'
At any cost, and haudin', the fugitive
Grace that alane can fetch, oor glisks o't teach,
  Genius within reach.

Afore each sovereign feat the swimmer maun
Gang under, and hoo many times, and oft
The source o' inspiration's ill to trace.
Still, still, we see it, infinitely aloft,
And struggle on—but gin oor poo'ers gi'e oot
  What will ha'en struggled boot?

A line, a word,—and emptiness again!
The impotent desire to ken aince mair
The shinin' presence, and the bitter sense
O' bein' unjustly treated, wi' despair
Cryin' 'better to see and tine, no' see ava'
  Like maist men'—ah!

This thocht o' a' wha haena had a glisk
And canna understand oor torments syne

Gie's courage to us—and the lust to bring
Like cruelties to them, tho' we ken fine
The veritable vision withdrawn alane
    Can gi'e (no justify) the pain.

No' justify, tho' we maun think it does
Or be indifferent to its effects,
Or wi' oor peers, or but oorsels, concerned,
Yet ken hoo genius a' oor themes rejects,
Syne gars the heavens open apropos
    'God' or the sea or Uncle Joe.

A'thing is equal here, and only here,
And ony o' my relatives may be
Occasions for genius. Let me look again.
A'thing is equal here—sae faur's we see—
Yet genius fa's unequally, here and there,
    And nane kens when nor where.

Juist as frae ony couple genius springs,
There is nae tellin' save wi' folk owre auld
Or impotent. The stupidest pair on earth
Are still as likely to strike in the blin' fauld
Maze o' man-seed upon the vital spark
    As folk o' merit, means, or mark.

Wanted a technique for genius! Or, at least,
A means whereby a' genius yet has done
'll be the stertin' point o' a' men's lives,
No' zero, as if life had scarce begun,
But to owrecome this death sae faur ben in
Maist folk needs the full floo'er o' Lenin.

Be this the measure o' oor will to bring
Like cruelty to a' men—nocht else'll dae;
The source o' inspiration drooned in bluid
If need be, owre and owre, until its ray
Strengthens in a' forever or's hailly gane
    As noo save in an antrin brain.

THE TERRIBLE CRYSTAL

To Sadie MacLellan (*Mrs Walter Pritchard*)

Clear thought is the quintessence of human life.
In the end its acid power will disintegrate
All the force and flummery of current passions and pretences,
Eat the life out of every false loyalty and craven creed
And bite its way through to a world of light and truth.

Give me the open and unbiased mind
Valuing truth above all prepossessions to such an extent
As to be ready to discard them all
τό κατ' 'Ανθρωπόν, and, furthermore,
Is content to approach Metaphysics through Physics,
In the Aristotlean sense in so far
As it recognises that empirical factuality
Can best be attested in that domain,
And is therefore impelled to recognise in the cosmos
A dynamic and teleological character

And by virtue of that recognition
Stands not far from religion
—A teleology essentially immanent,
God's relation to the world being in some general way
Like the relation of our minds to our bodies.
This is the hidden and lambent core I seek.
Like crystal it is hidden deep
And only to be found by those
Who will dig deep.
Like crystal it is formed by cataclysm and central fires;
Like crystal it gathers into an icy unity
And a gem-like transparence
All the colour and fire of life;
Like crystal it concentrates and irradiates light;
Like crystal it endures.

Since only those who have looked upon tragedy
Can dare to behold it.
It is terrible to uninitiated eyes.

Yet in this white stone
Those upon whom tragedy and catastrophe are come
May find their cure and their redemption,
For it has been formed in tragedy
And calcined in catastrophe
I have seen refractions of its purity
In the facets of seers past and present—
Virgil's day-star dawning over ruined Ilium;
Kierkegaard's 'arousal broad awake'
Out of his 'dread and trembling';
Barth's 'horizon light' breaking through the dark obscure;
Brunner's lightning flashes in the midnight of 'eclipse';
Heim's 'two infinitudes' beyond the boundary of dimension,

—Visions of a transcendental country
Stretching out athwart the temporal frontiers;
The sacrificial 'salutation of the cleanness of death'
On the part of Joan the Maid
—All, indeed, but broken lights,
Partial gleams reflecting each in their degree
Some aspect of the white intensity
Of that single central radiance,
But all carrying the same gospel:
'When consciousness is crucified upon circumstance
Give praise!'

The poetry I seek must therefore have the power
Of fusing the discordant qualities of experience,
Of mixing moods, and holding together opposites,
And well I know that the various facets
Of sensibility, sensuous, mental, and emotional,
And its alternating moods
Cannot be fully reconciled
Save in an imaginative integrity
That includes, but transcends, sensibility as such.
Our time opposes such integrity
As much as it demands it
And to struggle through complexity to simplicity
Is therefore as necessary as it is difficult.

A VISION OF SCOTLAND

I SEE my Scotland now, a puzzle
Passing the normal of her sex, going erect
Unscathed through fire, keeping her virtue
Where temptation works with violence, walking bravely,
Offering loyalty and demanding respect.

Every now and again in a girl like you,
Even in the streets of Glasgow or Dundee,
She throws her headsquare off and a mass
Of authentic flaxen hair is revealed,
Fine spun as newly-retted fibres
On a sunlit Irish bleaching field.

LARKING DALLIER

Up frae the sea the trusting rocks
You had nae suner wiled than you
Let oot a laugh and 'neth the wave
    Hid your ain sel' frae view.

The cheated rocks nae faurer cam'
Yet couldna to the deeps return
And day by day maun thole to watch
    Your same toom promise burn.

Tho' by the moon at second-hand
You drag the waters still you'll see
Nae mair dry land come snoovin' oot
    This side Eternity.

You conjure the larks, no continents,
And gar them soar and sing—but ah!
You'll no' even hear the burdies oot
    Afore you jouk awa'.

Men keep their feet upon the grun'
Tho' whiles their thochts the larks ootsoar,
For sense frae life's nae ither ploy
    Than light frae night afore.

Tho' subtler forms o' life emerge
They still maun cry: 'Nicht sune obscures
What profit's in ootsoarin' yet
    A' ither larks but yours!'

s

ESPLUMEOIR

'It was an amazing discovery, like the inside of your head
 being painlessly scraped out. There was an amazing clarity,
 like the brilliant moon falling into it and filling it neatly.'

'The utter stillness o' the timeless world,'
The haill creation has vanished forever
Wi nae mair noise or disturbance than a movie fade-out.

Naething to see—you sudna ha'e far to gang
For an analogy frae your Earth experience tho'.
Sin' at winter's edge when a'thing's gane sere
Toomed o' a' Simmer's routh and bare as a bane gey near
Bacteriologists say the soil's teemin' mair thrang
Wi' life than at ony ither time, wi' nocht to show.

'Aloof as a politician
The first year efter election,'
You grumble, 'There's naething to see.'

It's a' expressionless as tho' it micht be
Enamelled wi' an airbrush yon tawnish grey
Nae colour sae common on motors—was't only yesterday?—
Yet bright as when the stars were glowin'
Wi' sic a steady radiance that the lift
Seemed fu' to owreflowin'. I wadna hae't in a gift.
It mak's me feel upon my word
Like a fly on the edge of a phonograph record.'
(A phrase divertin'ly *vergeistigt* here!)

Eternity is like an auld green parrot
I kent aince. Its conversational range was sma'
Yet when it tilted its heid and cocked
A beady eye at you, you got the feelin'
That, gin it but chose, it could tell you a thing or twa;
That, as the French pit it,
Il connut le dessous des cartes.

34

Or like cricket's deceptive impression o' slowness
Tho' the split second decisions sae often required
Ha'e to be made quicker than in ony ither game;
Or as a day that was ga'en to be
Oppressively het wi' thunder later
Used to egg-on a'thing to live
Brimmin'ly afore the cataclysm.
Till a'thing that ran or flew or crawled
Abune or alow was filled pang-fu' wi' life
Like yon cicada shrillin' piercin'ly
Ettlin' to stert up the haill chorus.
He'd been undergrund an 'oor ago
And micht be doon a bird's throat by nicht.
That he was alive richt then was reason eneuch
For singin' wi' a' his micht.

Eternity's like that—a'thing keyed up
To the heichest pitch as if
A cataclysm's comin'—only it's no'!

Or pit it like this—Eternity
Is twa doors in frae the corner a'where,
A sma', demure, white buildin'
Wi' shutters and a canopy.
The canopy is royal blue
And it says *Eternity*
In discreet soap-glass letters
On ilka side. Under the canopy
You walk up and the front door
Is a' mirror wi' a cool strip
O' fluorescent licht on top.

You push the pearl button
And listen to the delicate chimes
And adjust your tie in the mirror
And fix your hat—but the guy
Ahint the bullet-proof mirror
Sees a' that tae,
Only you canna see him.

35

The guy ahint the mirror
Is Tutti-Frutti-Forgle,
A muckle nigger wi' fuzzy-white hair
Wha kens his business.
Aince past Tutti you check your hat
In a quiet soft-lit anteroom.
And the haill place is yours.

ON A RAISED BEACH

To James H. Whyte

ALL is lithogenesis—or lochia,
Carpolite fruit of the forbidden tree,
Stones blacker than any in the Caaba,
Cream-coloured caen-stone, chatoyant pieces,
Celadon and corbeau, bistre and beige,
Glaucous, hoar, enfouldered, cyathiform,
Making mere faculae of the sun and moon,
I study you glout and gloss, but have
No cadrans to adjust you with, and turn again
From optik to haptik and like a blind man run
My fingers over you, arris by arris, burr by burr,
Slickensides, truité, rugas, foveoles,
Bringing my aesthesia in vain to bear,
An angle-titch to all your corrugations and coigns,
Hatched foraminous cabo-rilieva of the world,
Diectic, fiducial stones, chiliad by chiliad
What bricole piled you here, stupendous cairn?
What artist poses the Earth écorché thus,
Pillar of creation angouled in me?
What eburnation augments you with men's bones,
Every energumen an Endymion yet?
All the other stones are in this haecceity it seems,
But where is the Christophanic rock that moved?
What Cabirian song from this catasta comes?

Deep conviction or preference can seldom
Find direct terms in which to express itself.
Today on this shingle shelf
I understand this pensive reluctance so well,
This not discommendable obstinacy,
These contrivances of an inexpressive critical feeling,
These stones with their resolve that Creation shall not be
Injured by iconoclasts and quacks. Nothing has stirred
Since I lay down this morning an eternity ago
But one bird. The widest open door is the least liable to intrusion,

37

Ubiquitous as the sunlight, unfrequented as the sun.
The inward gates of a bird are always open.
It does not know how to shut them.
That is the secret of its song,
But whether any man's are ajar is doubtful.
I look at these stones and know little about them,
But I know their gates are open too,
Always open, far longer open, than any bird's can be,
That every one of them has had its gates wide open far longer
Than all birds put together, let alone humanity,
Though through them no man can see,
No man nor anything more recently born than themselves
And that is everything else on the Earth.
I too lying here have dismissed all else.
Bread from stones is my sole and desperate dearth,
From stones, which are to the Earth as to the sunlight
Is the naked sun which is for no man's sight.
I would scorn to cry to any easier audience
Or, having cried, to lack patience to await the response.
I am no more indifferent or ill-disposed to life than death is;
I would fain accept it all completely as the soil does;
Already I feel all that can perish perishing in me
As so much has perished and all will yet perish in these stones.
I must begin with these stones as the world began.

Shall I come to a bird quicker than the world's course ran?
      To a bird, and to myself, a man?
      And what if I do, and further?
I shall only have gone a little way to go back again
And be like a fleeting deceit of development,
Iconoclasts, quacks. So these stones have dismissed
All but all of evolution, unmoved by it,
(Is there anything to come they will not likewise dismiss?)
As the essential life of mankind in the mass
Is the same as their earliest ancestors yet.

Actual physical conflict or psychological warfare
      Incidental to love or food
Brings out animal life's bolder and more brilliant patterns

Concealed as a rule in habitude.
There is a sudden revelation of colour,
The protrusion of a crest.
The expansion of an ornament,
—But no general principle can be guessed
From these flashing fragments we are seeing,
These foam-bells on the hidden currents of being.
The bodies of animals are visible substances
And must therefore have colour and shape, in the first place
Depending on chemical composition, physical structure, mode of
growth,
Psychological rhythms and other factors in the case,
But their purposive function is another question.
Brilliant-hued animals hide away in the ocean deeps;
The mole has a rich sexual colouring in due season
Under the ground; nearly every beast keeps
Brighter colours inside it than outside.
What the seen shows is never anything to what it's designed to hide,
The red blood which makes the beauty of a maiden's cheek
Is as red under a gorilla's pigmented and hairy face.
Varied forms and functions though life may seem to have shown
They all come back to the likeness of stone,
So to the intervening stages we can best find a clue
In what we all came from and return to.
There are no twirly bits in this ground bass.

We must be humble. We are so easily baffled by appearances
And do not realize that these stones are one with the stars.
It makes no difference to them whether they are high or low,
Mountain peak or ocean floor, palace, or pigsty.
There are plenty of ruined buildings in the world but no ruined stones.
No visitor comes from the stars
But is the same as they are.
—Nay, it is easy to find a spontaneity here,
An adjustment to life, an ability
To ride it easily, akin to 'the buoyant
Prelapsarian naturalness of a country girl
Laughing in the sun, not passion-rent,
But sensing in the bound of her breasts vigours to come

Powered to make her one with the stream of earthlife round her'
But not yet as my Muse is, with this ampler scope,
This more divine rhythm, wholly at one
With the earth, riding the Heavens with it, as the stones do
And all soon must.
But it is wrong to indulge in these illustrations
Instead of just accepting the stones.
It is a paltry business to try to drag down
The arduous furor of the stones to the futile imaginings of men,
To all that fears to grow roots into the common earth,
As it soon must, lest it be chilled to the core,
As it will be—and none the worse for that.
Impatience is a poor qualification for immortality.
Hot blood is of no use in dealing with eternity,
It is seldom that promises or even realizations
Can sustain a clear and searching gaze.
But an emotion chilled is an emotion controlled;
This is the road leading to certainty,
Reasoned planning for the time when reason can no longer avail.
It is essential to know the chill of all the objections
That come creeping into the mind, the battle between opposing ideas
Which gives the victory to the strongest and most universal
Over all others, and to wage it to the end
With increasing freedom, precision, and detachment
A detachment that shocks our instincts and ridicules our desires.
All else in the world cancels out, equal, capable
Of being replaced by other things (even as all the ideas
That madden men now must lose their potency in a few years
And be replaced by others—even as all the religions,
All the material sacrifices and moral restraints,
That in twenty thousand years have brought us no nearer to God
Are irrelevant to the ordered adjustments
Out of reach of perceptive understanding
Forever taking place on the Earth and in the unthinkable regions
                                                    around it;
This cat's cradle of life; this reality volatile yet determined;
This intense vibration in the stones
That makes them seem immobile to us)
But the world cannot dispense with the stones.

They alone are not redundant. Nothing can replace them
Except a new creation of God.

I must get into this stone world now.
Ratchel, striae, relationships of tesserae,
    Innumerable shades of grey,
    Innumerable shapes,
And beneath them all a stupendous unity,
Infinite movement visibly defending itself
Against all the assaults of weather and water,
Simultaneously mobilized at full strength
At every point of the universal front,
    Always at the pitch of its powers,
    The foundation and end of all life.
I try them with the old Norn words—hraun
Duss, rønis, queedaruns, kollyarum;
They hvarf from me in all directions
Over the hurdifell—klett, millya, hellya, hellyina bretta,
Hellyina wheeda, hellyina grø, bakka, ayre,—
    And lay my world in kolgref.

This is no heap of broken images.
Let men find the faith that builds mountains
Before they seek the faith that moves them. Men cannot hope
To survive the fall of the mountains
Which they will no more see than they saw their rise
Unless they are more concentrated and determined,
Truer to themselves and with more to be true to,
Than those stones, and as inerrable as they are.
Their sole concern is that what can be shaken
Shall be shaken and disappear
And only the unshakable be left.
What hardihood in any man has part or parcel in the latter?
It is necessary to make a stand and maintain it forever.
These stones go through Man, straight to God, if there is one.
What have they not gone through already?
Empires, civilization, aeons. Only in them
If in anything, can His creations confront Him.
They came so far out of the water and halted forever.

That larking dallier, the sun, has only been able to play
With superficial by-products since;
The moon moves the waters backwards and forwards,
But the stones cannot be lured an inch farther
Either on this side of eternity or the other.
Who thinks God is easier to know than they are?
Trying to reach men any more, any otherwise, than they are?
These stones will reach us long before we reach them.
Cold, undistracted, eternal and sublime.
They will stem all the torrents of vicissitude forever
With a more than Roman peace.
Death is a physical horror to me no more.
I am prepared with everything else to share
Sunshine and darkness and wind and rain
And life and death bare as these rocks though it be
In whatever order nature may decree,
But, not indifferent to the struggle yet
Nor to the ataraxia I might get
By fatalism, a deeper issue see
Than these, or suicide, here confronting me.
It is reality that is at stake.
Being and non-being with equal weapons here
Confront each other for it, non-being unseen
But always on the point, it seems, of showing clear,
Though its reserved contagion may breed
This fancy too in my still susceptible head
And then by its own hidden movement lead
Me as by aesthetic vision to the supposed
Point where by death's logic everything is recomposed,
Object and image one, from their severance freed,
As I sometimes, still wrongly, feel 'twixt this storm beach and me.
What happens to us
Is irrelevant to the world's geology
But what happens to the world's geology
Is not irrelevant to us.
We must reconcile ourselves to the stones,
Not the stones to us.
Here a man must shed the encumbrances that muffle
Contact with elemental things, the subtleties

That seem inseparable from a humane life, and go apart
Into a simple and sterner, more beautiful and more impressive world,
Austerely intoxicating; the first draught is overpowering;
Few survive it. It fills me with a sense of perfect form,
The end seen from the beginning, as in a song.
It is no song that conveys the feeling
That there is no reason why it should ever stop,
But the kindred form I am conscious of here
Is the beginning and end of the world,
The unsearchable masterpiece, the music of the spheres,
Alpha and Omega, the Omnific Word.
These stones have the silence of supreme creative power,
The direct and undisturbed way of working
Which alone leads to greatness.
What experience has any man crystallized,
What weight of conviction accumulated,
What depth of life suddenly seen entire
In some nigh supernatural moment
And made a symbol and lived up to
With such resolution, such Spartan impassivity?
It is a frenzied and chaotic age,
Like a growth of weeds on the site of a demolished building.
How shall we set ourselves against it,
Imperturbable, inscrutable, in the world and yet not in it,
Silent under the torments it inflicts upon us,
      With a constant centre,
With a single inspiration, foundations firm and invariable;
      By what immense exercise of will,
Inconceivable discipline, courage and endurance,
      Self-purification and anti-humanity,
         Be ourselves without interruption,
            Adamantine and inexorable?
It will be ever increasingly necessary to find
In the interests of all mankind
Men capable of rejecting all that all other men
      Think, as a stone remains
Essential to the world, inseparable from it,
      And rejects all other life yet.
Great work cannot be combined with surrender to the crowd.

—Nay, the truth we seek is as free
From all yet thought as a stone from humanity.
Here where there is neither haze nor hesitation
Something at least of the necessary power has entered into me.
I have still to see any manifestation of the human spirit
That is worthy of a moment's longer exemption than it gets
From petrifaction again—to get out if it can.
All is lithogenesis—or lochia;
And I can desire nothing better,
An immense familiarity with other men's imaginings
Convinces me that they cannot either
(If they could, it would be instantly be granted
—The present order must continue till then)
Though, of course, I still keep an open mind,
A mind as open as the grave.
You may say that the truth cannot be crushed out,
That the weight of the whole world may be tumbled on it,
And yet, in puny, distorted, phantasmal shapes albeit,
It will braird again; it will force its way up
Through unexpectable fissures? look over this beach.
What ruderal and rupestrine growth is here?
What crop confirming any credulities?
Conjure a fescue to teach me with from this
And I will listen to you, but until then
Listen to me—Truth is not crushed;
It crushes, gorgonizes all else into itself.
The trouble is to know it when you see it?
You will have no trouble with it when you do.
Do not argue with me. Argue with these stones.
Truth has no trouble in knowing itself.
This is it. The hard fact. The inoppugnable reality,
Here is something for you to digest.
Eat this and we'll see what appetite you have left
For a world hereafter.
I pledge you in the first and last crusta,
The rocks rattling in the bead-proof seas.

O we of little faith,
As romanticists viewed the philistinism of their days

As final and were prone to set over against it
Infinite longing rather than manly will—
Nay, as all thinkers and writers find
The indifference of the masses of mankind,—
So are most men with any stone yet,
Even those who juggle with lapidary's, mason's, geologist's words
      And all their knowledge of stones in vain,
Tho' these stones have far more differences in colour, shape, and size
      Than most men to my eyes—
Even those who develop precise conceptions to immense distances.
      Out of these bleak surfaces.
All human culture is a Goliath to fall
To the least of these pebbles withal.
A certain weight will be added yet
To the arguments of even the most foolish
And all who speak glibly may rest assured
That to better their oratory they will have the whole earth
For a Demosthenean pebble to roll in their mouths.

I am enamoured of the desert at last,
The abode of supreme serenity is necessarily a desert.
My disposition is towards spiritual issues
Made inhumanly clear; I will have nothing interposed
Between my sensitiveness and the barren but beautiful reality;
The deadly clarity of this 'seeing of a hungry man'
Only traces of a fever passing over my vision
Will vary, troubling it indeed, but troubling it only
In such a way that it becomes for a moment
Superhumanly, menacingly clear—the reflection
Of a brightness through a burning crystal.
A culture demands leisure and leisure presupposes
A self-determined rhythm of life; the capacity for solitude
Is its test; by that the desert knows us.
It is not a question of escaping from life
But the reverse—a question of acquiring the power
To exercise the loneliness, the independence, of stones,
And that only (come)s from knowing that our function remains
However isolated we seem, fundamental to life as theirs.
      We have lost the grounds of our being,

45

We have not built on rock.
Thinking of all the higher zones
Confronting the spirit of man I know they are bare
Of all so-called culture as any stone here;
Not so much of all literature survives
As any wisp of scriota that thrives
On a rock—(interesting though it may seem to be
As de Bary's and Schwendener's discovery
Of the dual nature of lichens, the partnership,
Symbiosis, of a particular fungus and particular alga).
    I grasp one of them and I have in my grip
The beginning and the end of the world,
My own self, and as before I never saw
The empty hand of my brother man,
The humanity no culture has reached, the mob.
Intelligentsia, our impossible and imperative job!

'Ah!' you say, 'if only one of these stones would move
—Were it only an inch—of its own accord.
    This is the resurrection we await,
—The stone rolled away from the tomb of the Lord.
    I know there is no weight in infinite space,
        No impermeability in infinite time,
But it is as difficult to understand and have patience here
        As to know that the sublime
Is theirs no less than ours, no less confined
To men than men's to a few men, the stars of their kind.'
        (The masses too have begged bread from stones,
        From human stones, including themselves,
      And only got it, not from their fellow-men,
      But from stones such as these here—if then.)
Detached intellectuals, not one stone will move,
Not the least of them, not a fraction of an inch. It is not
      The reality of life that is hard to know.
It is nearest of all and easiest to grasp,
But you must participate in it to proclaim it.
—I lift a stone; it is the meaning of life I clasp
Which is death, for that is the meaning of death;
How else does any man yet participate

In the life of a stone,
How else can any man yet become
Sufficiently at one with creation, sufficiently alone,
Till as the stone that covers him he lies dumb
And the stone at the mouth of his grave is not overthrown?
—Each of these stones on this raised beach,
        Every stone in the world,
Covers infinite death, beyond the reach
Of the dead it hides; and cannot be hurled
Aside yet to let any of them come forth, as love
        Once made a stone move
    (Though I do not depend on that
        My case to prove).
So let us beware of death; the stones will have
Their revenge; we have lost all approach to them,
But soon we shall become as those we have betrayed,
And they will seal us fast in our graves
As our indifference and ignorance seals them;
        But let us not be afraid to die.
No heavier and colder and quieter then,
No more motionless, do stones lie
        In death than in life to all men.
It is no more difficult in death than here
—Though slow as the stones the powers develop
To rise from the grave—to get a life worth having;
And in death—unlike life—we lose nothing that is truly ours.

Diallage of the world's debate, and of the long auxesis,
Although no ébrillade of Pegasus can here avail,
I prefer your enchorial characters—the futhorc of the future—
To the hieroglyphics of all the other forms of Nature.
Song, your apprentice encrinite, seems to sweep
The Heavens with a last entrochal movement;
And, with the same word that began it, closes
Earth's vast epanadiplosis.

IN TALK WITH DONNCHADH BÀN MAC AN T'SAOIR[1]

After making an English verse translation of his *Moladh Beinn Dobhrain*

NOT the speech of ordinary city folk (with their air
Of elaborate superciliousness which testifies
To ages of systematic half-culture. They seem
To utter that hopeless word *connu*). But in such wise
As Doughty found in the poorest Arabians—the bird-like ease
Alacrity and perspicuous propriety of speech
United with quick significance—since words must reach
To the heart of the matter, like Abdullah of Keybar's
'Round kind of utterance, with election of words,
And dropping with the sap of human life,'
Or the young man of Shuggera's, who put life in his words
As a juggler impresses his will on his properties:
An art learnt not from books but from life—tales of men
Unlettered like you, yet wise in speech, and practised, like you,
(Aye, even to the mental grasp of a Rob Donn
Whose *Oran a' Gheamhraidh* is an exact counterpart,
Line by line and phrase by phrase,
Of Alexander MacDonald's *Oran an t-Samhraidh*,
Tho' he could not read the original on which he wrought!
—Greater even than Su Tungp'o's feat of writing
A complete set of poems on the rhymes used
By the complete poems of T'ao).
Not town-folk's speech, flat like the rest of their natures,
But the power that can speak to the heart of others
With that faculty of sheer description
Which not only tells *what* a thing is, but at least
Incidentally goes far towards telling *why*.
—But beyond this how? The speech of one neither man nor animal—
                                                    or both—
Yet not monster; a being in whom both races meet

[1] Donnchadh Bàn Mac An T'Saoir (Duncan Bàn MacIntyre), 1724–1812, one of the greatest of Scottish Gaelic poets, was a deer-stalker, unable to read or write, who carried all his poems in his head until towards the end of his life he dictated them, amounting to several thousands of lines, to a minister friend.

On friendly ground—all the pleasantness of sylvan life,
All the genial and happy characteristics of creatures
That dwell in woods and fields, seeming mingled and kneaded
Into one substance with the kindred qualities in human nature,
Trees, grass, flowers, streams, cattle, deer and unsophisticated man,
Like a poet's reminiscence of the time
When man's affinity with nature was more strict
And his fellowship with every living thing more intimate and dear,
Like the Faun of Praxiteles—not supernatural,
Just on the verge of nature yet within it.
Nature needed, and still needs, this beautiful creature
Standing betwixt man and animal, sympathising with each,
Comprehending the speech of either race, and interpreting
The whole existence of one to the other.
—How happy such a life, enjoying the warm, sensuous,
Earthy side of Nature, revelling in the merriment of woods and streams,
Living as our four-footed kindred do—as mankind did
In its innocent childhood before sin or sorrow
Or mortality itself had been thought of! How difficult to make out
A genius such as yours. So full of animal life as you were,
So joyous in deportment, so handsome, so physically well-developed,
Giving no impression of incompleteness, of maimed or stinted nature,
Yet in literary intercourse how we
(Educated chimpanzees, O thou Gaelic Mozart!)
Habitually and instinctively allow for you
As for a child or some other lawless being,
Exacting no strict obedience to conventional rules,
Hardly noticing your eccentricities enough to pardon them
Because of the indefinable characteristic that sets you outside our
                                                            bounds,
(You who were writing superb descriptions
Of wild scenery for its own sake
When the English were still complaining
Of the 'frightful irregularity' of Highland mountains,
'Most of all disagreeable when the heather is in bloom'
And making pained contrast of them
With that truly 'poetical mountain', Richmond Hill!
It was not until the success of Scott and Wordsworth
Your attitude could be conceived of by the South of England.

4

In an age of brilliant Gaelic poetry, Scottish Lowlanders even
Regarded the Highlanders as illiterate savages
And the sad history of Highland education
In the three centuries after 1560
Reveals they did their best to make them so)
—The Faun—twenty-five centuries old, to judge by the date
Praxiteles carved on this statue; oh, Donnchadh Bàn,
A century and a half by Scottish literary history,
You look as young as ever; you have nothing to do with time,
But have the look of eternal youth in your face . . .
It would be relatively easy to write the history
Of a pair of nesting dab-chicks or of a day in their life,
With a continuousness and exhaustiveness that might challenge
                                                    comparison,
Without breaks, a seamless garment,
With the most accomplished and most dangerous works of modern
                                                    fiction,
Differing from them only in not pretending to know
The birds' minds from the inside out, but hoping at best
To get at their nature from their movements and write their odyssey
By working from the outside in; but the red deer are more difficult
                                                    subjects
Than any species of birds, since there is in their existence
No period of helplessness—nothing to correspond
To the nesting season and its ties.—Even the new-dropped calf
Needs little or no attention from its mother,
In its first days of weakness, she suckles it
But twice in twenty-four hours, and as soon as it needs her more
It is already able to follow her wherever she goes.

How can we expect ever to know with accuracy then
The life and movements of individual deer?—At the best a man
Who has seen an immense number of typical incidents
Might nigh to the end of a long life get near telling us
What the probable main outlines of the story would be.
Without intuitional divination all the tests and checks
Of science avail nothing. The desire to be with them,
Near them, among them must be a controlling passion.

Your long life was a more or less continuous stalk.
This brought you nearer to their life than any other poet
(Even we who have pursued everything appertaining to deer
So closely that we have not even missed
The fact that in the Gospel of Teliau,
Now commonly known as the Book of St. Chad
There is a stab in St. Matthew xii, 48,
Between *bo* and *nos*, and in this hole
The deer's hair from the original skin can still be seen.
Even the photostat shows the mark
Where the hair is in the stab.)

The whole threshold of awareness was raised; the whole organism
Worked with unheard-of co-ordination. It is almost
As if to know the life of a deer one must become a deer
And live among them; and as your life showed
That is not so impossible as it may sound.
You got near enough to such an imaginative identification
To know that your life and theirs were part of one plan.
The deer are more than the material of a scientist's paper.
Indeed the nobility of their beauty has been
Among the major motives of poetry since time began,
And the mere sight of a stag in its wild freedom still
Means more to many of us than to hear the nightingale's song.
—But only in *your* poetry can we feel we stand
Some snowy November evening under the birch-trees
By a tributary burn that flows
Into the remote and lovely Dundonnell river
And receive the most intimate, most initiating experience,
When three hinds and a stag approach where we stand,
Rise on their hind legs, and browse on the twigs above us.
We could touch them; their breath comes into our faces.
Many more of the herd are within a few yards of us.
We have the feeling of having reached that state
All watchers of animals desire
Of having dispensed with our physical presence.
Or is that it? Is not really the bottom of our desire
Not to be ignored but to be accepted? . . .

51

ONCE IN A CORNISH GARDEN

(For Valda)

'A spray of red rose berries flung against the blue
Cornish sky—what more does man want here below ?'
STEPHEN MCKENNA

'Even as St. John could not depict
The glories of the New Jerusalem without
Recourse to gold and precious stones, so we
Our spirits' perfect state in terms
Of Cornish geology.'

'Il y a deux sortes d'élaborations géologiques: L'une qui est un procès de désintégration: le granit, par exemple, qui devient argile. L'autre—et c'est comme le philosophe qui, par le brassage d'une multitude de faits, arrive au concept, au joyau abstrait d'une définition irréprochable—est une espèce de création ou de parturition, quelque chose à quoi aboutir qui échappe à la décomposition par la simplicité. Les entrailles de la nature en travail ont enfanté ce bézoard. Il a fallu la presse cosmique, l'action qui est passion d'un monde en révolte contre sa propre inertie, l'épreinte tellurique, le vomissement du feu intérieur, ce qui de plus central est capable de jaillir sous une main inexorable, l'écrasement millénaire de ses couches qui se compénètrent, tout le mystère, toute l'usine métamorphique, pour aboutir à ce brillant, à ce cristal sacré, à cette noix parfaite et translucide qui échappe à la pourriture du brou. Parfaite, pas encore! Il faut que la main de l'homme s'ajoute à ce caillou qui l'invite. Il faut qu'un lent polissage vienne dissiper l'obscurité inhérente, effacer la rugosité adventice, accentuer le clivage, éliminer le défaut, éveiller l'œil secret, compléter la rose ébauchée. Il faut que la facette multiplie le prisme. Il faut user le refus. Il faut que naisse ce prodige minéral qui est un nombre solide; il faut qu'apparaisse enfin sous la main de l'ouvrier ce soleil minuscule qui doit ses rayons à la géométrie. (Ainsi cette pierre merveilleuse dont parle Buffon, et que j'aime autant ne pas identifier, et qu'il appelle la girasol.) Non plus un miroir seulement, mais un foyer.'

PAUL CLAUDEL, *La Mystique des Pierres Précieuses*

THERE is no outline of the landscape here.
No element in the objective world,
You have not vitalised for me,
(*Sprys Kernow*,[1] be with me now!)
At every turn establishing some original confrontation
Of Cornwall and myself as pure and as immediate
As on Creation's day.
And how you suit your setting at every point!
Cornwall incarnate, costumed by Aage Thaarup,
With your little nigger felt cap, its forward poke
Accentuated by fringed grosgrain ribbon;
Dress and coat in the new Persian brown,
The coat generously trimmed with lamb to tone,
And with large antique bronze buttons
To finish the draped neckline of the dress.
Or, at night, in 'Nitchevo', the little Ardanse black crepe dress,
Its intricate and unusual cut blazoned by
A waistcoat-bodice of white and gold lamé.
These are your colours—sultan-red, rich gold, gold brown,
Black, scarlet, nut-brown and sunrise pink,
Copper glance, purple, peach, and cream,
Cherry, geranium, coral flame, and blush,
Wheat gold, sun-orange, and harlequin red,
Just as the right cosmetic chart for your type is this—
Carmine rouge, used high on the cheeks and skilfully shaded;
Brown eye-shadow; black eyelash make-up;
Black eyebrow pencil very carefully applied
Not to give a harsh line;
A rachelle powder, dusted lightly over
To soften the whole make-up; carmine lip-stick,
And a rachelle make-up blender for your arms and neck;
And for the evening under artificial lights
You'll change your powder to the flesh colour
And your eye-shadow to a glorious violet
And use vermilion lip-stick.
Even as in our garden all the flowers have
Colours like these and look
Like isolated moods of yours, particular memories of you,

[1] Cornish Gaelic, meaning 'Spirit of Cornwall'.

Gestures and smiles of yours that have somehow taken root
And flourish here for ever.
Oh, all the colour in this golden moment
Seems to flow from you!
—The brilliant red supergiant El Monte asters,
Double petunias in fringed, ruffled, and laciniate forms,
Rose of Heaven and Little Star petunias,
And, among the roses, the flaming yellow
And copper-toned Feu Fernet-Ducher, the coral-petalled
Carillon, and the brilliant deep-red Dickson's Centennial.
Then the sweet-scented Golden Gleam nasturtiums,
The great clusters of glorious fiery red Russian lilies,
—Like the reflection of my own heart's blood—
And the rainbow show of giant zinnias
Burnt orange, deep salmon, rose and purple
And these be your words, beloved,
In so far as earth-speech may avail,
That sight or sound of you always
May conjure up without fail—
Coinnealta, solasta, croidhearg, cunbalach,
Eireachdail, taiceil, gloir-ghleasta, fionfhuil, gniomb-luaineach,[1]
And for the phrase that matches you best
'The mile-great sheaf-like blast of purple-glowing and red flames'
Or Meredith's 'her pomp of glorious hues, her revelry of ripeness,
                                                    her kind smile',
The 'radiance rare and fathomless'
That Hardy won in Cornwall too
(Doughty loved Cornwall and spent his honeymoon here,
And W. H. Hudson, and Stephen McKenna,
The translator of Plotinus—even as I!)
Best of all the little knit play-suit you made yourself
Of peau d'ange yarn, shorts of corn yellow,
Stripped short-sleeved jumper blouse of corn yellow and brown,
And brown knit overskirt to button on to the shorts
When you want to be less informal,
Or that other one, dusty pink flannel skirt,
Matching high-necked sweater blouse,

[1] These Scottish Gaelic words mean bright, brilliant, blood-red, constant, hand-some, staunch, of tuneful speech, of deft deed, and 'wine-blood' (i.e. noble).

And prune-coloured knitted finger-tip jacket,
The belt of the blouse prune suede.
Or your Tahitian *paréo*, with its gay printed shorts and brassiere,
And skirt open down the front
—A new high note in hilarity!
Caprice Espagnol earrings of little carved red roosters,
Or, again, lattice sandals of black satin
Studded with mirror baguettes,
A tiny black felt jockey cap with huge bunches of black aigrettes
Jumping out at unexpected places at the front and sides;
And the house things you have chosen
(Ah! The blond wood, and pistachio and rose-red upholstery,
And great vase of crimson-black Nigrette hybrid tea-roses!
—Rare examples of Swedish sloyd, beautiful
Hand-beaten pewter-ware and delicately blown
Mountain glass so frail that it looks
Like curly white smoke, and peasant rugs
From Dalecarlia, striped in orange and red and purple!)
Or on windy promontories or in the autumn lanes
In your wine-red suit of rough soft woollen
With a mushroom-collar of beaver, blouse and coat-lining
Of a wool shell-knit fabric in a shade of blue
That looks shimmery because two different tones are used.
I have a million memories of you, all fitty and suant.[1]
From waters like the Dancers of Huai Nan,
(Chang Hang's famous poem . . . 'So dance to dance
Endlessly they weave, break off and dance again
Now flutter their cuffs like a great bird in flight,
Now toss their long white sleeves like whirling snow')
And the dark-green rocks with bands of grey felspar or yellow epidote,
(Scryrer meyn,[2] be with me now!)
Through all the intensely plicated, compressed, cleaved series
To the 'Delabole Butterfly', the clear blue topaz at Cigga and
                                                    St. Michael's Mount,
The wolfram openworks at the north end of Bodmin Moor
(Not Wolfram's—von Eschenbach's—too little opened works,
Which, though lip-service is occasionally paid

[1] Cornish words meaning appropriate and sweetly satisfying.
[2] Cornish, meaning reader of the rocks.

To the conventional *amour courtois*, find
The true relation between man and woman in the married state
—In this a marrow of the *Song of Winifreda*
A kindred spirit wrote two hundred years before.
Poets of happy married life are few, and none,
Not even Patmore, meets the case for me—
And portray a Parzival not as a lad who wins
By reason of his utter purity and innocence
To the beatific vision but a boy who, brought up
In complete ignorance of life, is driven
By his innate force of character to go out
Into the world to carve his career and achieves
Success only after many misadventures due
To his lack of experience and failure to grasp
The true spirit of chivalry; I, too have failed
The suffering Amfortas more than once,
And, proving incompetent in Grail Castle,
Been driven out into the world again
And spent much time in Trevizent's company
—Excuse a parenthesis like Wolfram's own!)
The Tremore elvan spangled with purple fluorspar
(Which Derbyshire workers call Blue John), [1]
The pinitiferous elvan at Goldsithney,
The Prah Sands elvan, and the flow-banded
Quartz felsite of Tregonetha.
And we are with the Cornish miners and we know
'Horses' from 'vughs', 'peach' from 'capel' or 'gozzan' from 'iron hat',
The 'pigs' eggs' of the clay-workers, and whether China stones
Are 'hard purple', 'mild purple', 'hard white' or 'mild white'.
The Goss Moors and the Luxulyan valley,
St. Nectan's Kieve, the Rocky Valley, Lydford Gorge and Lustleigh
Cleave
Are all known to us, and we have loved to note
The grey and purple fine-grained compact basalt
Of the Dunchideoch type, and where the red Iddingsite occurs,
Dolomitic conglomerate in the Keuper Series,
Metamorphic aureoles round the granite masses
And subangular stones of quartzite, grit and quartz

[1] John, i.e. Jaune.

56

In a dark red matrix of sand, and the peculiar
Red quartz-porphyry in the breccias between Dunchideoch and Ide,
And all the herring-boned or chevroned pegmatite dykes
And those inclusions of the iron front driven by potassium,
And later, silica, into enclaves (like the Cornish people themselves)
That form the dark ovoid patches the quarrymen
Call 'furreners' in the coarse granite.
And changes of volcanic rocks abutting on granite
Into calcereous hornfels, showing the minerals
Axinite, vesuvianite, and garnet.
Extensive sheets of spilitic lava and of tuff
With beds of radiolarian chert, the large
Amygdaloidal and pumiceous masses of Brent Tor,
The horneblends picrite of Polyphant ornamental stone,
And, in the albite-diabases, augite fresh and purplish hued
In ophitic enclosure of the albite laths,
And all the upward sequence of lithological types
Extending from Lewannick to Trevalga.
White quartzite *schuppen* of Gorram Haven
Connected with the Breton and Portuguese fauna,
Networks of ilmenite and prisms of apatite,
Lenses of dark blue limestone, groups of sheared dolerite sills,
Shining plates of enstatite or bastite, facaoidal masses
Of pink and grey gneiss in the serpentine, north-west of Kennack,
Dykes of gabbro in the serpentine near Coverack,
And flaser structure developed as at Carrick Luz.
The meneage rocks of the Lizard and the Start and Bolt,
The Ordovician rocks at Manaccan, Veryan, and Gorram Haven,
The Mylor and Portscatho Beds—we know them all,
And every scovan, every stannary, and all
The greywethers of Cornwall, the sarsden-stone,
And piles of attal-Sarsen, Jews' leavings,
And stringers and stockwerks, greisens and gangue,
'Black shell' and 'stent', 'grizzle' and 'growder',
The Cretaceous Overstep, the Cowstones, and the Foxmould sands,
Horneblende, in the extreme stages of contact alteration,
Pale-brown with large crystals or entirely acicular,
With needles so fine that they are referred
To horneblende only by analogy.

57

Or the decomposed mica-lamprophyres of Newquay Headland and
the Gannel,
And fresh biotite-orthoclase traps like the Hicksmill and Lemail Dykes,
We know them all, all bathed in the glow of unison
Or in the frail effulgence of eternity.
Hence here we can perceive contentedly,
Abreast of the attempt to synthesize
Work on the soil sciences with that
On the ductless glands,
The fact that sexual selection was originally directed
Mainly by the need to economise iodine,
The whole development, physical and mental of our race
Dependent on the supply of certain minerals in the soil,
And all our instinct closely associated with
The unconscious desire for particular kinds of food,
And face without fear the future phosphorous shortage
That will not immediately reduce our numbers, but at first
Swell them to well-nigh Oriental proportions.
And as the theory that the foliation of the Lizard rocks
Was due to injection foliation in a metasomatic rock
Was followed by that of dynamism and orogeny
Till it was found that these structures could only be created
By *both* these agencies acting concurrently,
So through the whole range of possible experience
In our intelligence, intuitions, thoughts and beings
We know we are able *recompenser* each other
—Recompenser in French philosophy's use of the term,
Or as a watchmaker would use it of his wheels and escapement!
(Though if our relation like that between body and mind
Is not described as one of interaction
It is mainly because that word does not express
Adequately the intimate character of the relation)—
Without fear, although we clearly realize
Perpetual mental progress is neither impossible nor inevitable.
Clear thought is the quintessence of human life.
In the end its acid power will disintegrate
All the force and flummery of current passions and pretences,
Eat the life out of every false loyalty and craven creed,
And bite its way through to a world of light and truth.

DEPTH AND THE CHTHONIAN IMAGE

On looking at a ruined mill and thinking of
the greatest

(*To John Macnair Reid*)

Absolvitur ab instantia is decreed
In every case against you men array.
Yours is the only nature stiflin' nocht,
Meetin' a' the experiences there are to ha'e
And never meetin' ane o' them raw-edged.
Ripe, reconcilin' mind, sublimely gauged,
Serene receptiveness, nae tongue can speak
Your fair fey form felicitously enow,
Nae subtle mind seek your benmaist howe
And gar your deepest implications beek.
The mills o' God grind sma', but they
In you maun crumble imperceptibly tae.
Nor shadowed nor lit up by ony thocht,
Nae perfect shinin' o' a simmer's day
Vies wi' your ark's assopat speed
In its pure task engaged.
Time and Eternity are no' at odds
In you as in a' that's Man's—and God's,
For nane can look through you as through the sun and see
Some auld adhantare wi' neuked bonnet there,
Urphanömen—o' what? Ah, no, alluterlie
You deal afflufe wi' a' that's fordel and nae gair
In your allryn activity lets kyth
      The faur-side o' your sneith.

As life to death, as man to God, sae stands
This ruined mill to your great aumrie then,
This ruined mill—and every rinnin' mill?
The awte or bait o' everything you ken
And tak' it quicker than a barber's knife
Wi' nocht aclite. There is nae chance o' strife.

Micht a' the canny your abandon see!
Nor ony din they mak' let them forget
Their generations tae and creeds'll yet
Crine to a sic-like laroch while the lets-a-be
O' a' your pairts as eidently agree.
Nocht needs your wa's mair audience to gi'e.
Forever ample baith in scouth and skill,
Watchin' your aws by nicht it seems to me
The stars adreigh mimic their drops and 'mang hands
There is nae nearer image gi'en to life
O' that conclusive power by which you rin
Even on, drawin' a' the universe in,
Than this loose simile o' the heavenly hosts
Vainly prefigurin' the unseen jaups
Roond your vast wheel—or mair waesome ghosts
O' that reality man's pairt o' and yet caps
Wi' Gods in his ain likeness drawn
            —Puir travesties o' your plan.

To picture the invisible via the stars
Is the least boutgate that man's speech can gang,
As for your speed and your boon millin'—no' even the lang
Processes o' metamorphosis in rock
Can fetch that ben to him like the shadowy flock
O' atoms in himsel' precariously seen,
Queer dirlin' o' his cells at sic an 'oor,
He whiles can note wha hasna else the poo'er,
Laichest Brownian movements swarmin' to his een
As neath a microscope—a deemless thrang,
To catch their changin' time, and get the hang
O' a' their swift diminishments doon the steep
Chutes o' dissolution, as he lay amang
The mools already, and watched the maggots' wars
Upon his flesh, and sune its finitude mock
Their midgeswarm jaws until their numbers fa'
To a'e toom mou', the fremit last o' a'
The reelin' corruption, its vain mudgeons there
Wi' motions that nae measure can seize on
As micht the sun to earth's last look appear

Like yon cart-wheel that raxes to a cone
Afore the spider lets its anchorage slip,
      An insect in its grip.

Nae knowledge its ain offices here
Can seek to magnify and ithers suppress.
An arbiter frae corruption free hauds sway
Unlike man's mind that canna ken unless
It decks its data wi' interpretation
To try to mak' a rational creation.
Hence a' men see contains faur mair than's seen,
Remembrance o' the past, fancy o' the future.
To memory and imagination you stand neuter
As 'twere a scientist confrontin' the gi'en
That nae logical, *a priori*, or ither reasons confess
And yet are carriers o' value that redress
His rational world frae bein' senseless tae,
Tho' here, as in sma'er things, nae inspired guess,
Teleological reasonin' or rapport sheer,
Gi'es minds like his sic valuable dilation.
You're no' its meanin' but the world itsel'.
Yet let nae man think he can see you better
By concentratin' on your aneness either.
He pits his mind into a double fetter
Wha hauds this airt or that, no baith thegither.
You are at aince the road a' croods ha' gane
      And alane wi' the alane.

Alane wi' the alane, yet let us no' forget
Theistic faiths but, extrapolate, plottin' on
The curve o' sae-ca'd knowledge science has made
—Science and theism ha'e their roots in common
(Tho' few can credit sic a teachin' noo!)—
And needs the same redress as sciences do
To say the least. Alane wi' the alane remains
A relative conception as self-betrayed
As heidstrang science dispensin' wi' sic aid
As frae the world's allogic, kept in mind, it gains.
Nae mutual justice, undue claims foregone,

Sympathy wi' divers ootlooks and endeavours shown,
Union o' knowledge's kingdoms piously prayed,
Is less a movement leadin' awa' frae you
Than ony in the opposite airt to it,
Nor can a poet as I am cease to con,
Heedless o' baith, your prime significance
To lead his muse a needle-angel's dance
By hailin' truth a mathematical point
Wi' nae relation to the ooter world,
Whether the times are in or oot o' joint
O' scant concern since a'thing earthly's hurled
—You tae—indifferent, *adiaphora*, faur alow
      Ocht this taks' heed o'.

Aye balk and burral lie the fields o' life.
It fails to acresce a kennin' frae the past,
In a' its fancied contacts wi' what's meant
When it seems shairest in worst backspangs cast;
Its heritage but a bairn's pairt o' gear,
A puir balapat at hairst its fingers speir
And often mairket a toom barley-box;
Aye in bad breid despite their constant toil,
As bairns in their bairnliness, a cursed coil
Hauds men content wi' casual sweetie-pokes
O' a' creation's gear; and little is amassed
Maist folk can life-rent—nocht hain at last.
Yet o' the way-drawn profit wha tak's tent?
The feast is spread yet helplessly they fast,
Aye win an Irishman's rise wi' unco strife,
Cast oot frae a' their dues by the silly fear
That hauds them in habits o' poortith still,
While by them brim the torrents to your mill,
The vast way-drawing that denies mankind
Or pairt or parcel in science or in art
Till bare as worms the feck o' them we find.
Each generation at zero still maun start
And's doomed to end there, wi' a' that they forgaed
      Caught in the suction o' your lade.

Or pairt or parcel in science or in art.
—Or even in life! Hoo few men ever live
And what wee local lives at best they ha'e.
Sirse, science and art might weel rin through the sieve,
Or jow like backfa's when the mill is set.
If maist folk through nae elf-bores dribbled yet
But in some measure lived to a' life is.
Wad that their latent poo'ers 'ud loup alist,
Kyth suddenly a' their wasted past has missed,
And nae mair leave their lives like languages,
—Mere leaks frae streamin' consciousness as if
Thocht roon' itsel' raised wa's prohibitive
O' a' but a fraction o' its possible sway—
But rax in freedom, nocht inhibitive,
In fearless flourishin' amidwart,
Fed by the haill wide world and feedin' it,
Universal life, like an autonymous tongue
In which some vision o' you micht be sung,
Let us remove a' lets and hindrances then
Even as the principle o' limitation, God,
Packed wi' posterity, silent like the deid,
And aye respondin' to a lesser need,
Has vanished like a clood that weighed on men
Owre lang—till your pure radiance glowed.

Ein Mann aus dem Volke—weel I ken
Nae man or movement's worth a damn unless
The movement 'ud gang on withoot him if
He de'ed the morn. Wherefore in you I bless
My sense o' the greatest man can typify
And universalise himsel' maist fully by.
Nocht ta'en at second-hand and nocht let drift,
Nae bull owre big to tackle by the horns,
Nae chance owre sma' for freedom's sake he scorns,
But a' creation through himsel' maun sift
Even as you, nor possible defeat confess,
Forever poised and apt in his address;
Save at this pitch nae man can truly live.
Hence to these ruins I maun needs regress

—As to the facts o' death and a' the past again,
Beast life, plant life, minerals, water, sky,
A' that has been, is, is to be—frae you
Clear seen, still clearer sicht to pursue.
Similia similibus rotantur, a' facts amang
I seek the *ereigniswerden*'s essence then
That shows a' that seems kent in it wrang
And gars a' else point back to it again,
Their worth to guide wha can use them hence
        To your fulfillin' experience.

Elschaddai. Emelachan. We only want
The world to live and feel its life in us?
But the world lives whether we dae' or no',
A's vice that abates life or can blin' us
To your final epopteia—contents us with
The hearin' o' the ear, no' the vision swith,
The life o' shadows, mere tautology,
Ony curious fig-leaf o' the mind whereby
Humanity has socht to hide its sin,
Portentuous prison-hooses o' fause thocht we see
'Science' big heicher daily—a' that can pin us
To the spectral frae the live world, come atween us
And the terrible crystal, the ineffable glow.
Diseases o' the will that needs maun fin' us
Less potent to act, and a' the clichés and cant,
Limitations o' personality, pap for pith,
Robotisation, feminism, youth movements,
A' the super-economic programme's intents
Set grey, a hellish parody (oot there
Forenenst your blazin' energy), and its
Perpetual fause alarms, shams o' seemin' fair,
Fixed fallacies auld as man, sheer waste o' wits
—Oh, you are no' the glory mankind desires
        Yet naething else inspires!

The recurrent vividness o' licht and water
Through every earthly change o' mood or scene
Puirly prefigures you—a' Nature's dreamt,

64

And no' dune, thrang wi' 'ither plans, has been
A fog twixt you and us. It's nocht to ken
Something has happened—save only when
'Mang mony alternatives sic choice was ta'en.
You aye exclude a' ither possibilities.
A'e voice may cry alood: 'Wha ever sees
You to hairy goon and mossy cell has gane.'
Anither proclaim the vital vision gi'en
'Ud move to deeds frae care o' consequence clean.
But baith are wrang—the reckless and the fremt.
And in your radiant licht man's first truth's seen
—Tho' still the last and least to matter
In a' their fond affairs to the mass o' men—
The love o' economics is the mainspring
O' a' the virtues. Eternity like a ring,
Virile, masculine, abandoned at nae turn
To enervatin' luxury
Aboot me here shall ever clearer burn,
And in its licht perchance at last men'll see
Wi' the best works o' art, as wi' you tae,
        Chance can ha's nocht to dae!

THE ROYAL STAG

The hornless hart carries off the harem.
Magnificent antlers are nothing in love.
Great tines are only a drawback and danger
To the noble stag that must bear them.

Crowned as with an oaktree he goes,
A sacrifice for the ruck of his race,
Knowing full well that his towering points
Single him out, a mark for his foes.

Yet no polled head's triumphs since the world began
In love and war have made a high heart thrill
Like the sight of a Royal with its Rights and Crockets,
Its Pearls, and Beam, and Span.

GLOSSARY

Abune	*above*	Bawbees	*half-pennies*
Aclite	*awry*	Beek	*shine brightly*
Acresce	*increase*	Ben	*through*
Adhantare	*phantom*	Benmaist	*inmost*
Adreigh	*distant*	Bides	*awaits*
A'e	*one*	Birks	*birch trees*
Afflufe	*extemporary*	Birsled	*scorched*
Afore	*before*	Blackie	*blackbird*
Ahint	*behind*	Blainy	*blemished*
Ain	*own*	Blanderin'	*babbling*
Aiblins	*perhaps*	Blauds	*fragments*
Airt	*this direction*	Blin'	*blind*
Allryn	*weird*	Bluid	*blood*
Alluterlie	*utterly*	Boon	*excellent*
Alow	*below*	Boot	*matter*
Alist	*alive*	Bourach	*cluster*
Antrin	*occasional*	Boutgate	*roundabout way*
Armits	*earth-nut*	Bowzie	*misshapen*
Arselins	*backwards*	Brairds	*grows*
Areness	*oneness*	Breeks	*trousers*
Assopat	*drudging*	Buirdly	*stalwart, well-*
Aumrie	*cupboard*		*made*
Awa'	*at all*	Burnal	*strip of barren*
Awn	*owes, owning*		*land*
Aws	*owning*		
Awte	*grain*	Coup	*upset*
		Crine	*shrink*
Backfa'	*side sluice of a*	Crockets	*tresses*
	mill	Cuit-deep	*ankle-deep*
Balapat	*a pot in a farm-*	Cundy	*drain*
	house for the		
	family but not	Da'	*dare*
	for the reapers	Dae	*do*
	in harvest	Deemless	*uncountable*
Balk	*ridge in ploughing*	Ding	*knock*
Bait	*grains*	Dirlin'	*throbbing*
Baith	*both*	Dung	*knocked*

67

Eidently	*eagerly*	Gundy	*violent*
Elf-bones	*hole in a piece of wood*	Ha'ein'	*having*
Ettlin'	*eager*	Hag	*peat*
		Haill	*whole*
Fa'	*fall*	Hain	*preserve*
Faddomed	*fathomed*	Hairst	*harvest*
Fash	*worry*	Hauds	*holds*
Fauld	*fold*	Hawdin'	*holding*
Fause	*false*	Heels-owre-gowdy	*head-over-heels*
Feck	*majority*	Heicher	*higher*
Fegs	*truly*	Heidstrang	*head-strong*
Fidged	*worried*	Herried	*plundered*
Fog-theekit	*moss-thatched*	Howe	*hollow*
Fordel	*progressive*	Hustle-farrant	*clad in tatters*
Forgaed	*gave up*		
Forhoolied	*abandoned*		
Fornenenst	*against*	Jaups	*splashes*
Fremit	*strange*	Jouk	*dodge*
Fug	*moss*	Jow	*surge*
Fullyery	*foliaged*		
		Kelterin'	*undulating*
Gaed	*went*	Ken	*know*
Gair	*small patch*	Kittle	*difficult*
Gane	*gone*	Knoul-taed	*swollen-toed*
Gang	*go*	Knurl	*knob*
Gar'd	*made*	Kyth	*become known*
Garded	*covered*		
Get	*illegitimate off-spring*	Lade	*mill stream*
Gi'en	*given*	Laicher	*lower*
Gin	*if*	Laichest	*lowest*
Glaur	*mud*	Lammergeir	*great hooded vulture*
Glisks	*glints*		
Gloghole	*deep hole*	Laroch	*hole in the ground*
Gowd'-bestreik	*gold-streaked*	Lave	*remainder*
Gowden	*golden*	Lear	*learning*
Grun'	*ground*	Leid	*language*
		Lift	*sky*

68

Louch	*come-hither*	Siller	*silver*
Loup	*leap*	Simmer	*summer*
Lown	*quiet*	Sirse	*exclamation of surprise*
Lugs	*ears*		
		Sma'-bookin'	*shrinking*
'Mang	*among*	Sma'er	*smaller*
Maun	*must*	Smirrs	*drizzle*
Mools	*soil for a grave*	Sneith	*smoothness*
Mou'	*mouth*	Snoovin'	*sneaking*
Muckle	*much, big*	Socht	*searched*
Mudgeons	*mocking motions*	Soupler	*supplier*
		Speir	*ask*
'Neth	*beneath*	Stell	*fix*
Neuked	*crooked*	Sune	*soon*
Nicht	*night*	Sweetie-	
Nocht	*nought*	pokes	*bags of sweets*
		Swith	*swift*
Ocht	*anything*	Syme	*then*
Pang-fu'	*crammed full*	Tak's tent	*takes care*
Ploys	*amusements*	Thegither	*together*
Poortith	*poverty*	Thole	*endure*
Puirness	*poorness*	Thrang	*busy*
		Tine	*lose*
Ramel	*branches*	Toom	*empty*
Raxes	*reaches out*	Trauchlin'	*troubling*
Rice	*branch*	Thraw	*throw*
Routh	*plenty*	Thrawart	*perverse*
		Thrawn	*stubborn*
Sae	*so*	Thridden	*threading*
Sae-ca'd	*so-called*		
Sair	*serve*	Waesome	*woeful*
Scho	*vascilate*	Wheesht	*quiet*
Sclaffer	*shuffle*	Whiles	*sometimes*
Scouth	*scope*	Wice	*wise*
Seggs	*insignificant plants*	Wud	*wood*
		Whummle	*upset*
Shairest	*surest*		
Sic-like	*such like*	Unco	*extraordinary*